SPACE MYSTERIES

WHAT ARE STARS MADE OF?

Gareth Stevens
PUBLISHING

BY JOAN STOLTMAN

Please visit our website, www.garethstevens.com. For a free color catalog of all our high-quality books, call toll free 1-800-542-2595 or fax 1-877-542-2596.

Library of Congress Cataloging-in-Publication Data

Names: Stoltman, Joan, author.
Title: What are stars made of? / Joan Stoltman.
Description: New York : Gareth Stevens Publishing, [2019] | Series: Space mysteries | Includes bibliographical references and index.
Identifiers: LCCN 2017054372| ISBN 9781538219553 (library bound) | ISBN 9781538219577 (pbk.) | ISBN 9781538219584 (6 pack)
Subjects: LCSH: Stars--Constitution--Juvenile literature. | Stars--Formation--Juvenile literature. | Stars--Evolution--Juvenile literature. | CYAC: Stars.
Classification: LCC QB808 .S76 2018 | DDC 523.8/6--dc23
LC record available at https://lccn.loc.gov/2017054372

Published in 2019 by
Gareth Stevens Publishing
111 East 14th Street, Suite 349
New York, NY 10003

Copyright © 2019 Gareth Stevens Publishing

Designer: Katelyn E. Reynolds
Editor: Joan Stoltman

Photo credits: Cover, p. 1 NASA/CXC/M. Weiss; cover, pp. 1, 3–32 (background texture) David M. Schrader/Shutterstock.com; pp. 3–32 (fun fact graphic) © iStockphoto.com/spxChrome; p. 5 NASA/JPL-Caltech; p. 7 NASA (http://www.nasa.gov/), ESA (http://www.spacetelescope.org/), and the Hubble Heritage (http://heritage.stsci.edu/) Team (STScI (http://www.stsci.edu/)/ AURA (http://www.auraastronomy.org/)); p. 9 Time Life Pictures/Jet Propulsion Laboratory/The LIFE Picture Collection/Getty Images; p. 11 NASA (http://www.nasa.gov/), ESA (http://www.spacetelescope.org/), and the Hubble Heritage (http://heritage. stsci.edu/) Team (STScI (http://www.stsci.edu/)/AURA (http://www.auraastronomy.org/))-ESA (http://www.spacetelescope. org/)/Hubble Collaboration; Acknowledgment: D. Gouliermis (Max Planck Institute for Astronomy, Heidelberg); p. 13 Skylines/ Shutterstock.com; p. 15 Oona Räisänen (User:Mysid), User:Mrsanitazier/Wikipedia.org; p. 17 NASA (http://www.nasa.gov), ESA (http://www.esa.int), Andrew Fruchter (STScI (http://www.stsci.edu)), and the ERO team (STScI + ST-ECF (http://www.stecf.org)); p. 18 X-ray: NASA/CXC/Morehead State Univ/T.Pannuti et al.; Optical: DSS; Infrared: NASA/JPL-Caltech; Radio: NRAO/VLA/ Argentinian Institute of Radioastronomy/G.Dubner; pp. 19, 29 NASA; p. 21 ESO/S. Steinhöfel/Wikipedia.org; p. 23 (Bunsen burner) ggw/Shutterstock.com; p. 23 (flames) IanRedding/Shutterstock.com; p. 25 (main) Julius Scheiner/Wikipedia.org; p. 25 (prism) radiorio/Shutterstock.com; p. 27 Bettmann/Getty Images.

Printed in the United States of America

CPSIA compliance information: Batch #CS18GS: For further information contact Gareth Stevens, New York, New York at 1-800-542-2595.

CONTENTS

Words in the glossary appear in **bold** type the first time they are used in the text.

WHAT IS A STAR?

There are billions of **galaxies** in outer space. Each one has billions of stars that live for billions of years. These stars are actually giant balls of hot gases with a **dense** core, or center.

Before learning about what stars are made of, you first have to understand their life cycle. Stars—like people, plants, and animals—go through several stages from birth to death. They're made of different elements at each stage!

OUT OF THIS WORLD!

Our galaxy is called the Milky Way. Scientists think around seven new stars are born in the Milky Way galaxy every year!

←our sun

CLOUDS OF DUST AND GAS

In space, **gravity** pulls together dust and gases to form huge cloudlike masses called nebulae. Most of the gas—about 90 percent—in a nebula is hydrogen. The other 10 percent is mostly helium. Small amounts of other elements are also mixed in.

Sometimes a nebula is stirred up by an event in space, such as a passing **comet**, and its dust and gases clump together. As the clumps become larger, their gravity grows, pulling in even more dust and gas.

OUT OF THIS WORLD!

Objects with greater mass have a stronger gravitational pull, and gravity is strongest between objects that are closer together. Earth's gravity is what keeps people from floating off into space!

This nebula, called the Crab Nebula, may one day form a new star!

PROTOSTARS

A nebula clump will eventually begin to spin and form a kind of disk. This disk spins faster and pulls in more dust and gas, creating a hot, solid core called a protostar.

A protostar will continue to grow and become hotter. It will eventually become so dense that its hydrogen atoms fuse, or join together, and become helium atoms. This action is called nuclear fusion. It's what gives stars their **energy**. A protostar will keep growing for millions of years.

OUT OF THIS WORLD!

Protostars have big clouds of dust surrounding them, which makes it impossible for scientists to see them through regular **telescopes**. They must use tools that "see" heat and light that people's eyes can't see!

The core is more dense than the rest of the star. This means its parts are very close together, and there's a lot of mass in a small space.

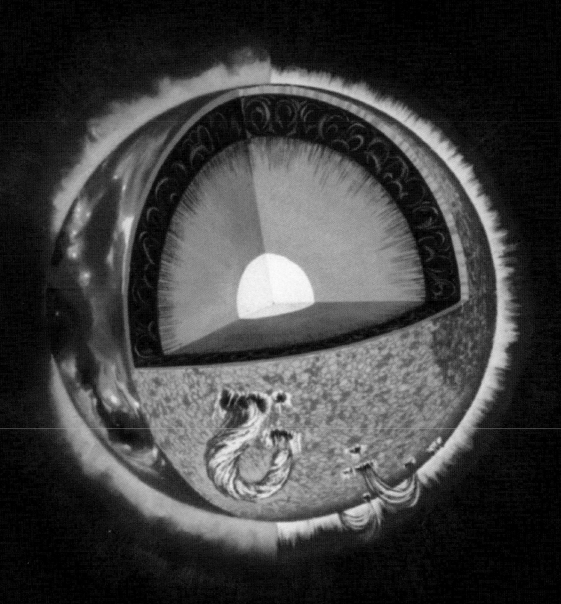

A STAR IS BORN!

Protostars are made up of hydrogen, helium, and space dust, just like the nebulae they came from. After a long time, when a protostar is large enough, its gravity will be overtaken by the force created by its nuclear fusion.

At this point, a blast of energy shoots from the north and south poles of the protostar, pushing away the remaining gas and dust. A star is born! The new star will use its remaining hydrogen as fuel for nuclear fusion.

OUT OF THIS WORLD!

A protostar that never has nuclear fusion happen is called a brown dwarf.

Nebulae start out at about −450°F (−268°C)! Eventually, a protostar can heat up to about 27 million°F (15 million°C).

THE MAIN SEQUENCE

After a star is born, it enters the longest and most **stable** part of its life: the main sequence. This stage can last billions of years, depending on a star's mass. The greater the mass, the hotter the core and the faster nuclear fusion changes hydrogen to helium.

During the main sequence, gravity tries to pull matter in and shrink the star while heat from nuclear fusion tries to make the star expand, or grow bigger. This creates a balance that keeps the star stable.

OUT OF THIS WORLD!

A star's helium is no different than the helium found on Earth. We use helium to make balloons float!

MAIN SEQUENCE STAR FACTS!

size	color	surface heat	lifetime	brightness
smallest	red	4,500°F (2,500°C)	200 billion years	least glow
↓	orange	7,000°F (4,000°C)	50 billion years	
	yellow	9,500°F (5,200°C)	10 billion years	
	yellowish-white	11,500°F (6,500°C)	3 billion years	↓
	white	15,500°F (8,500°C)	1 billion years	
	blue	35,500°F (20,000°C)	100 million years	
largest	blue	80,500°F (44,700°C)	10 million years	most glow

Stars in their main sequence are stable. That means they won't be exploding or dying any time soon!

BIG RED

After billions of years, the star has turned all its hydrogen into helium and nuclear fusion stops. Without fusion's heat to balance out gravity, the star collapses, or falls in on itself. After a while, gravity will start nuclear fusion again, though this time it fuses helium atoms together to make carbon atoms.

Helium fusion creates a lot of heat, so the star becomes huge. The outer **layer** of the star cools as it grows, so it turns a reddish color. The star has now reached its red giant stage.

OUT OF THIS WORLD!

The red giant stage lasts between 1,000 and 1 billion years, until all the helium is used up.

14

the sun as a red giant

the sun as a main sequence star

When the sun reaches its red giant stage,
it will be over 250 times its current size!

15

DEATH OF A STAR

For smaller stars, the outer layers are pushed away from the carbon core at the end of the red giant phase. This forms a cloud of gas called a planetary nebula. The carbon core stays in place and becomes a white dwarf star.

Larger stars grow and grow until they have so much mass they explode under their own gravity! This is called a supernova. Most of the star's mass is shot out into space, creating a new nebula where future stars may form!

OUT OF THIS WORLD!

White dwarfs are only about 1 percent as big as the sun, but they have about the same mass. This means they're very dense.

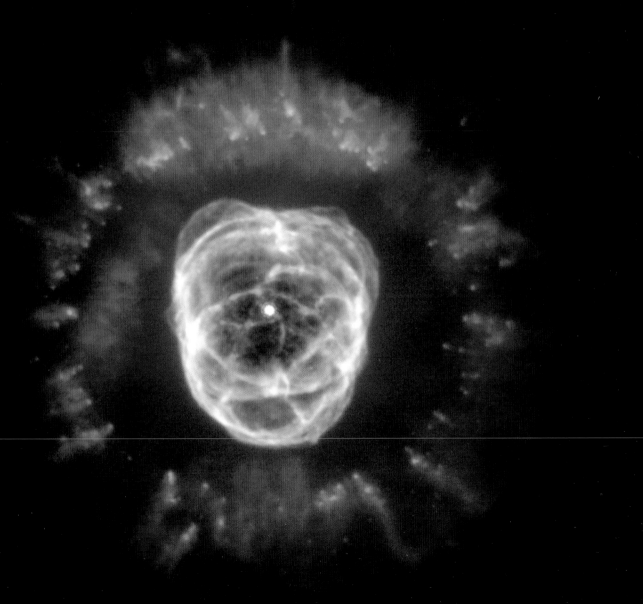

Planetary nebulae got their name because early **astronomers** thought they looked like **planets**. You can see the dying star in the center of the Eskimo Nebula.

SUPERNOVAS AND NEUTRON STARS

The explosions known as supernovas only last a few seconds, but they have so much force that nuclear fusion occurs! The nuclear fusion in supernovas makes many of the heavy elements found in the universe, such as copper, silver, and gold!

The core of a larger star may also collapse, forming a neutron star. Neutron stars are very dense. They can have twice the mass of our sun but only take up the space of a small city!

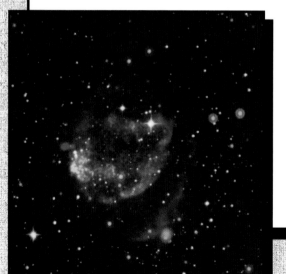
supernova

A black hole can form after a supernova if the remaining core is more than 2.5 times the mass of our sun. We don't know a lot about black holes, though, because nothing—not even light—can escape their gravity!

19

HERE COMES THE SUN

The most important star to us is the one that gives us daylight and the heat plants and animals need to live. It's the sun, and it's made of hydrogen and helium like every other star!

Don't worry, it won't be dying any time soon. The sun's main sequence still has 5 billion years to go. Then it will slowly turn into a red giant. Billions of years after that, it'll explode again and again until only a white dwarf remains.

OUT OF THIS WORLD!

Because our sun is pretty small compared to some stars, it won't explode into a supernova. Instead, it'll be a red giant and then a white dwarf for trillions of years.

white dwarf

From left to right, this picture shows how the sun grew into a yellow star and will one day become a red giant. On the far right, it shows how the sun will die, exploding again and again until all that's left is a tiny white dwarf.

21

HOW DO WE KNOW?

Nobody has ever visited a star—the spacecraft would melt! So how do astronomers know what stars are made of?

In 1860, scientists Robert Bunsen and Gustav Kirchhoff figured out that all elements give off a special pattern of colors, called a spectrum, when they burn. They took careful notes while burning each element. From then on, scientists could tell elements apart. This method of studying light became known as spectroscopy, and it's still used widely today. Scientists use spectroscopy to study stars!

OUT OF THIS WORLD!

Each spectrum pattern Bunsen and Kirchhoff discovered was unique, meaning it only belonged to one element.

Robert Bunsen developed this tool—the Bunsen burner—so he could see the colors given off by burned elements. These photos show the colors of a few elements and compounds as they burn.

cobalt

potassium

copper

sodium chloride

LOOKING AT LIGHT

To figure out what a star is made of, scientists simply need to compare the spectrums of known elements to the spectrums of light given off by a star. Studying elements in space isn't easy. Astronomers need special tools just to see a star!

Astronomers pass starlight through a telescope into a spectrometer, a tool that separates light into spectrums. Stars can have many elements—especially if they're older. Each spectrum must be carefully recorded so they can be compared to known spectrums later.

OUT OF THIS WORLD!

Stars have so much light energy they can be seen millions of miles away. This is why we can study them from Earth!

Spectroscopy is one of the most important tools in **astronomy**. Scientists also use it to figure out the density and temperature of objects in space.

A COOL CATALOG

Natalie Hinkel is a scientist who studies what stars are made of. In 2014, after 2 years of hard work, she shared the Hypatia Catalog with the world.

The Hypatia Catalog organizes, or sorts, the large amounts of **data** scientists have collected for almost 6,000 stars near the sun. It includes facts and figures for about 50 elements found in these stars! The catalog also notes the location, age, and more for certain stars. Using the Hypatia Catalog, scientists can compare stars in great detail!

Hypatia was one of the earliest women known to study astronomy.

MORE TO LEARN!

There's still so much scientists want to know about stars! NASA hopes to soon send a space probe, or unmanned spacecraft, to study the sun, which is the closest star to Earth. No probe has ever gotten within 4 million miles (6.4 million km) of the surface of the sun. Maybe one day we'll be able to take a closer look!

People who study stars often work at schools, laboratories, or NASA. Maybe you'll study stars at one of these places someday!

OUT OF THIS WORLD!

People who study nuclear fusion for a living are called nuclear physicists. They often work at schools or laboratories.

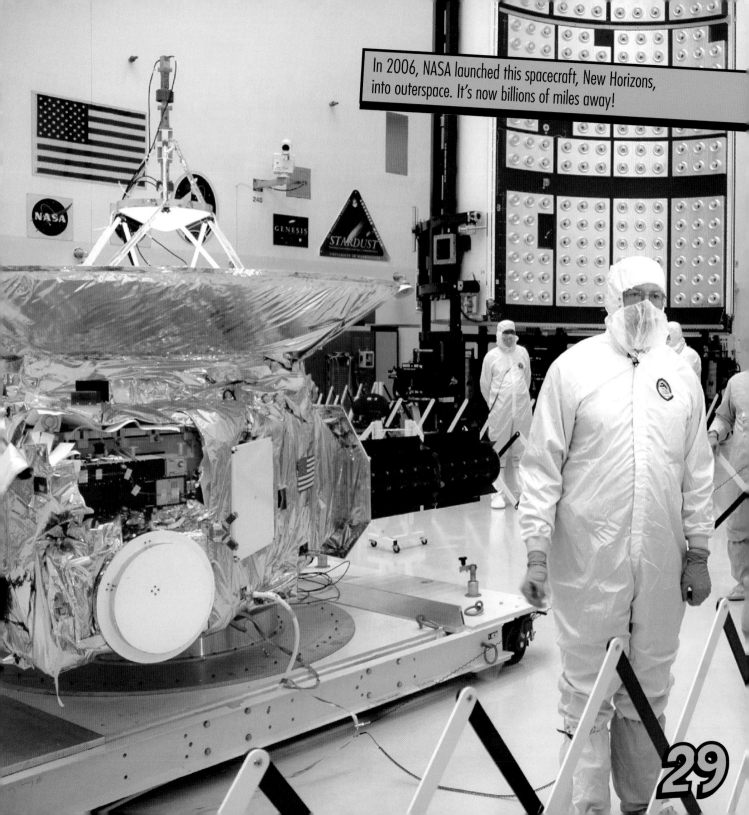

In 2006, NASA launched this spacecraft, New Horizons, into outerspace. It's now billions of miles away!

29

GLOSSARY

astronomer: a person who studies stars, planets, and other heavenly bodies

astronomy: the study of outer space

comet: a space object made of ice and dust that has a long glowing tail when it passes close to the sun

data: facts and figures

dense: packed very closely together

energy: power used to do work

galaxy: a large group of stars, gas, planets, and dust that form a unit within the universe

gravity: the force that pulls objects toward the center of a planet or star

layer: one thickness of something lying over or under another

planet: a large, round object in space that travels around a star

stable: not likely to change suddenly or greatly

telescope: a tool that makes faraway objects look bigger and closer

FOR MORE INFORMATION

BOOKS

Abramson, Andra Serlin and Mordecai-Mark Mac Low. *Inside Stars*. New York, NY: Sterling Children's Books, 2011.

Nandi, Ishani and Caroline Bingham. *First Space Encyclopedia*. New York, NY: DK Publishing, 2016.

Sparrow, Giles. *The Sun and Stars*. Mankato, MN: Smart Apple Media, 2012.

WEBSITES

Periodic Table and the Elements
www.chem4kids.com/files/elem_intro.html
This site explains each element with useful pictures and text.

Space Explained: What Are Stars and Planets Made Of?
www.telegraph.co.uk/science/2016/03/22/space-explained-what-are-stars-and-planets-made-ofsolar/
Watch this short video to learn more about stars!

INDEX